FAMOUS AMERICAN INDIAN LEADERS

WOLF OF THE DESERT
The story of Geronimo

Written by: Jill C. Wheeler
Edited by Paul J. Deegan

1

Published by Abdo & Daughters, 6537 Cecilia Circle, Bloomington, Minnesota 55435

Library bound edition distributed by Rockbottom Books, Pentagon Tower, P.O. Box 36036, Minneapolis, Minnesota 55435

Library of Congress Number: 89-084911   ISBN: 0-939179-68-7

Cover Photo by: Bettmann Archive
Illustrations by: Liz Dodson

War was a way of life for the Apache (uh PACH EE) Indians. Throughout the Southwest, the name Apache was enough to make men, women and children shiver in terror. Few sounds stop the heart like the Apache war cry howling through the morning stillness. The Apache raids were always swift and fierce. They lasted only minutes but left a trail of destruction which became their mark. The fiercest leader of them all was Geronimo. When younger, he had been known as Goyathlay.

"It's over," the medicine man said. His hand gently closed the now sightless eyes of Goyathlay's father. The young Apache boy's glance rested on his father's still motionless face for a moment. Then it moved solemnly to the eyes of his mother. She was seated across from him in the smoky wickiup. From now on, it would be his responsibilty to protect her. He also would have to hunt for food for her, and for his brothers and sisters.

Goyathlay rose to his feet and moved silently out of the round brush hut. He stopped for a moment outside and gazed up at the blazing desert sun. His short, stocky body was tanned a deep red, the same color as the desert in which he lived. All Apaches were this way, and their coloring enabled them to blend in with the scrub and rocks on the desert floor. Enemy warrriors often had ridden within feet of an entire war party, but they had seen nothing until the war party chose to make its presence known.

Goyathlay was only nine years old, to young to participate in any raids, but his father had seen to it before he died that the boy would be well prepared when the time came. Already he could run all day in the desert sun with neither food nor water. He could bury the head of his arrow in a tree trunk at 30 paces, and he had killed many small game, as well as an antelope.

"What are you doing, yawning one?"

Goyathlay turned to see it was Natchez speaking to him. Goyathlay hated it when the other children made fun of his name. He had received the name because he had been such a sleepy baby.

"Are you dreaming of killing a panther now?" Natchez said. "Or will you kill a rat and pretend it is a mighty beast?"

"Be quiet!" Goyathlay said angrily. "You are just jealous that my arrows fly farther and my aim is more true than yours! I will be the greatest warrior in the Apache nation, you will see!"

With that, he stomped away from the boy and grabbed his bow and arrow from where they lay near the wickiup. He would practice some more. He would make his father proud. Was he not the grandson of the great Apache chief Maco?

Goyathlay watched the antelope tugging at the dry, desert grass. He lay in the bushes, his red-brown body blending in with the hot desert sand. He had been motionless for nearly an hour, waiting for the antelope he had been tracking since early that morning. Goyathlay was an expert tracker, able to pick up signs all the other Apache boys missed. He also had learned the art of patience from his father. Today, the wait would be worthwhile.

Whoosh!

His arrow cut silently through the shimmering heat, piercing the antelope's frail chest. It staggered and fell to the ground, only a few feet from his hiding place. Goyathlay waited for a moment, and when he was sure it was dead, he dragged it so its head faced the east and began to skin it.

He was careful as he worked to never step over the animal or walk in front of it. These steps were all part of the Apache way to butcher an animal. Butchering was just one of many daily activities guided by traditions and stories handed down through the centuries.

Goyathlay had been very young when he first heard the story of how his people came to be. Apaches were the children of Child of the Water. Child of the Water had a brother, Killer of Enemies. They were the sons of White-painted Woman. She was the first person created by Yusn Life-giver to inhabit the earth.

Child of the Water killed all the monsters, making it safe for the Apaches. He also laid down many rules, such as the laws of butchering. An animal

Goyathlay tracks an antelope.

must be butchered according to Apache law Child of the Water had said. Otherwise, bad luck would be cast over the next hunt.

Killer of Enemies, Goyathlay had learned, was the father of the whites. When the time had come for the two sons of White-painted Woman to choose weapons, Killer of Enemies had taken firearms and Child of the Water had picked bows and arrows. That, he was told, was why the whites were different.

Goyathlay finished skinning the animal and cut it up. He picked up his bundle of meat and scanned the desert floor for a pebble to put in his mouth. The rock would keep his mouth from drying out during the long run home. Something didn't feel right, and he wanted to return home as quickly as possible.

When he reached the camp, he knew something was wrong. His mother greeted him with anxious eyes, her mouth twisted in anger.

"I am thankful you are back," she said. "Five hundred of our people have been killed, massacred by the white man."

"It is time for revenge. It is time you hunt more than antelope."

The Apaches and Mexicans had been sworn enemies for many years. The Apaches had chased the Mexican settlers of what is now Arizona and New Mexico into Mexico. Fights between Mexicans and Apaches were frequent and bloody. However, they had never before been as bad as this tragedy.

Goyathlay was practicing with his bow and arrow when he heard the noise coming from his village. The headman had returned from the war council with the new Apache chief, Mangas Colorado.

Mangas was a giant man, more than six feet tall. He had called for the war council after the massacre to decide what must be done to avenge the deaths. Now the headman would relay what Mangas had proclaimed.

Goyathlay listened carefully as the elderly headman repeated the words of the great chief.

"Too many lives have been lost and too much power lost to attack now. We will wait until our numbers are strong and our power flows through us like the river. The next time, the Great Spirit will smile upon us as we avenge this great wrong."

"Go now, and return on the rising of the fourth sun. Bring with all boys above the age of 10 to train in the ways of war. They are the branches with which we will rebuild our people so that our enemies cannot drive us from our homeland!"

Goyathlay listened in fascination as the old headman repeated the chief's words. The boy's only disappointment was that he was only nine.

Later that evening, his mother took him aside.

"You must prepare to leave at the rising of the sun. You are young, but you are strong and cunning. You will kill many whites who would force us from our homes. I will tell the warriors you are old enough to go with them."

Goyathlay stared at his mother in astonishment. An Apache never lied — a lie was the greatest sin an Indian could commit.

"Yes, I will lie," she said as if reading his thoughts. "I have told you never to lie, and you must remember that. But 500 of our people are dead. One lie will not bring them back. But it will put a great warrior in the path of the whites as they seek to rush down from the mountains and destroy us."

"You must become a great chief and you must kill until our land is safe for you and your sons. Now sleep. The morning will be here soon."

For the next eight years, Goyathlay learned the ways of the warpath. At the age of 12, Goyathlay was allowed to begin training with the scouts. The training was long and grueling. It was designed to prepare the future warriors to face hunger, thirst and fatigue. The desert was their training ground, and it was a strong opponent.

From sunup to sundown, Goyathlay and the other boys were pushed to their limits. They ran through the scorching heat with no water. Their food was whatever they could find along the way. All the while they were expected to suffer in silence. An Apache warrior was not allowed to admit to pain.

The training also was intended to force the boys to learn the territory by heart. They came to know every mountain top and every landmark.

Goyathlay grew to know the desert like he knew his own flesh. The trainers would leave a trail for the groups of boys to find. Goyathlay's group was always the first to discover it.

Three years later, Goyathlay moved to the hunters camp high up in the mountains. It was here they received formal training in the use of knives, bows and arrows, and spears.

But the ultimate test of Goyathlay's skill and daring came not from another boy. One day he was returning from a hunt with the other boys, their warrior trainers at the rear of the group. He was picking his way over a craggy mountain path when he heard a snarl. Out of the corner of his eye, he saw the blurred shape of a panther as it leapt into the air toward him.

There was no time to think, no time to draw bow and arrow, only time to react. Goyathlay whipped out his knife and crouched as the sleek, muscular animal flew over him. He thrust his knife up in time to slash the animal's tender underbelly before it landed.

The panther screamed and went limp. Goyathlay lay in a stunned silence, grateful to be alive.

Goyathlay kills the mighty panther.

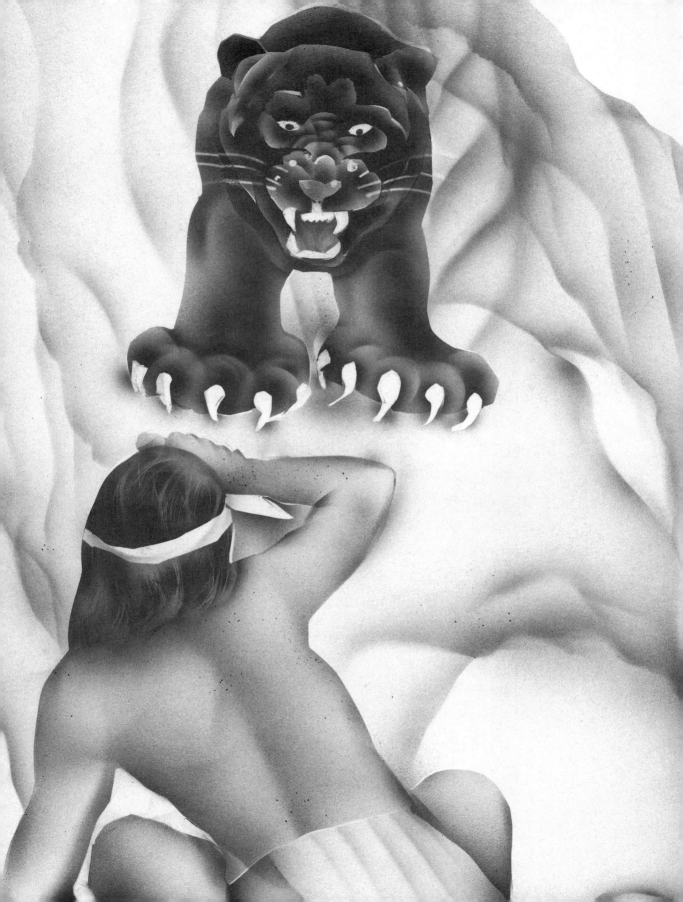

Hands pulled his bloody body away from the dead cat as the other boys stared in silence, awestruck by the fight they had witnessed. Goyathlay lurched back to camp in pain and triumph. He had bested the mighty beast singlehandedly in a hand-to-hand fight. Under the laws of the Apaches, he would now be able to join the warriors on the warpath.

Before an Apache boy could become a warrior, he had to go on the warpath four times with the other warriors from his tribe. On the warpath, he could not speak unless spoken to. He could only eat what he was given. He had to cook the food and care for the horses like a servant. He also had to learn the sacred names of everything on the warpath. No common names were used. Fear and pain were not allowed.

Goyathlay completed his four trips, and stood proudly before the warrior council. At the age of 17, he was the youngest boy upon whose head the great Mangas Colorado placed the warrior's band. From now on, he was Geronimo, Apache warrior.

Alope rocked back and forth on her knees as she scraped the hide from a deer her father had killed. When she finished scraping off the remaining flesh with her sharpened stone, she would soak it. Then, she would scrape off the hair and strech it in the sun to dry. It would make a handsome buckskin shirt for Geronimo, she thought.

She paused for a moment to look out across the desert, wondering where he was. Geronimo had said they could be married as soon as he became a warrior, but first he had to give her father, No-po-so, whatever he asked for. But No-po-so had said Geronimo must give him 20 horses to marry her — more than many warriors owned in a lifetime.

Alope sighed and went back to scraping the hide. They could never marry now. He might be able to steal four or five horses, but 20?.

She paused again to push her long, black braids out of her way. Listening carefully, she heard a mighty thundering in the distance. It sounded like a herd of animals. She squinted in the bright desert sun, finally picking out a tiny cloud of dust.

The cloud grew larger as the thundering increased. She stood up slowly and walked to the door of the wickiup she shared with her family. Her father met her at the doorway and followed her eyes to the horizon.

The lone horseman in the middle of the herd grew larger as he approached. Soon Alope was able to pick out Geronimo's face. It was him! And he had brought not 20 but 50 horses!

Alope's heart jumped as the warrior slid down from his horse and with a wave of his arm, presented No-po-so with the herd of horses. Without a word, he gathered Alope into his arms, swung her up on his horse and rode away. In the eyes of the tribe, they were now married. Geronimo had accomplished a feat no other warrior ever had, or ever would.

The next 12 years were happy ones for Geronimo and Alope. Geronimo continued to conduct

Geronimo claims Alope as his wife after bringing her father 50 horses.

daring raids across the border in Mexico. He returned heavily laden with plunder. His actions, and his bragging, earned him many enemies in the tribe. But he continued his raids in the hopes the tribe would recognize his right to be chief.

He and many of the other Apaches were unaware of the changes occurring across their homeland during those years. The Mexican War had been fought and won by the United States, and California and the Southwest now belonged to the Great White Father. Already soliders were tramping through Apache land on their way to California.

Mangas Colorado met with one of the white soldiers as the first troops made their way to California. He was told the Apaches, and their land, now belonged to the United States, and any Apache caught stealing from or harming an American would be killed. In addition, the Great White Father had promised the Mexicans that the Apaches would no longer raid their villages.

Geronimo and his band, however, were unaware of the promise, and they continued to cross the border to deal with the Mexicans. One summer, during a time of peace between the Mexicans and the Apaches, Geronimo's tribe crossed the border and camped in a Mexican town called Kas-ki-ye. During the day, the warriors would go to surrounding towns to trade. A small guard stayed at camp with the women and children.

Geronimo returned from trading one afternoon. He saw a small group of women and children staggering along the road from the camp. Their clothes were tattered and torn. Their faces were smudged with dirt and gunpowder.

"What is it? What has happened?" he asked them.

"The Mexicans came!" cried one of the women. "They killed all the guards and stole everything. Many others are dead, and we have no food or ponies left!"

Geronimo's wife, mother and his three small children were among the dead.

For three days, the broken warriors marched through the desert to their village. He burned the wickiup Alope had made and decorated for them. He also burned his children's toys and his mother's wickiup as well. His hatred of the Mexicans grew as high as the flames licking the dried sticks and brush. His anger was just as hot.

For the next few years, Geronimo and a small band of followers took their revenge against the Mexicans, raiding, plundering, killing, and burning. His name became linked to the lightning-swift raids which brought such destruction.

Chief Cochise (koh Chees) sat in stony silence, listening carefully to the interpreter. The white soldier was asking him to lay down his arms and move his people to a place the Great White Father would keep just for the Apaches, something he called a reservation. The Great White Father, the soldier continued, would give the Indians all the food and clothing they would need, and he would make sure the white settlers would leave them alone.

Cochise was in his 70s and his eyes were going bad, but he kept them fixed on the face of the soldier. He was trying to determine if he spoke the truth. Cochise looked away, staring across the distance at the land he loved so much.

Geronimo mourns the death of his wife and children.

Even the land, like the Apaches, was dying. The white settlers had killed most of the game. Food was scarce. Cochise knew his people would have to make peace with the whites or they would die.

"What is your answer?" the interpreter asked.

Cochise turned his gaze back to the soldier. He stood slowly and nodded, then turned to go tell his people. The war was over.

Geronimo's face was bright red with rage when he heard of Cochise's peace treaty with the whites.

"What chief would lay down his freedom to become a slave of the whites?" he asked his followers. "The whites are our enemies, we must fight them and use them as they have tried to use us!"

Geronimo stormed out of the council meeting he had been holding with his warriors. Now that Cochise had laid down his arms, only he and Chief Hoo were still on the warpath. It would be much harder for them to continue their raids now that they were alone, and the weak Apaches were put away, their every need being attended to by the whites. Geronimo still had to worry about the older members of his tribe, and the women and children.

Just outside the council meeting, a group of children were playing the moccasin game. The game was played by placing a bone in a moccasin and burying the moccasin with three empty ones. The children divided into teams and tried to guess which moccasin held the bone. Geronimo had played the game as a child.

Watching the children, he suddenly had an idea. Maybe he could make the whites see only what he wanted them to.

"Sure is amazing that ole Geronimo feller moved on to the reservation," the soldier told his companion. "Never thought they'd get that ornery injun to come here!"

"Me either," his friend said. "Wonder why he wanted to set up his camp right on the Mexican border?"

"Who knows. Probably reminds him of home or something. But you know, I never see him or his warriors. Just the old people and the women and kids. What do you think he does all day?"

"I wish I knew. Say, did you hear about the Mexican village 'cross the border that was raided the other day? Whoever did it knew what they were doing. Just came out of nowhere, stole 'em blind and disappeared in the desert. If I didn't know better I'd say it was..."

"Do you think?"

"No, it couldn't be. Could it?"

For two years, Geronimo conducted his lightning raids from a camp just across the border in Mexico while his people lived on the reservation. Unfortunately, the white's promises of food and clothing were hollow.

The Apaches had run out of choices. They could either starve on the reservation or go raiding and be hunted down by the whites. Geronimo chose the second option.

Geronimo and his warriors raided villages in Mexico.

At that time, a new, honest man came to run the reservation. Word of John Clum's kindness and fairness spread, and Apaches from throughout the desert came to live on the reservation under his rule. He even set up a court and police force of Apaches so the people could govern themselves.

Geronimo, however, preferred to remain on the warpath. The raiding continued, and the United States War Department ordered his arrest. The reservation officals decided to use the Apache police to help arrest one of their own.

Geronimo peered through his stolen field glasses. His scouts had informed him of the approach of a band of Apache police from the reservation. John Clum was leading the police to where Geronimo's warriors were camped. The camp was near a small settlement called Warm Springs. Another scout had told Geronimo that Clum wanted to speak with the Apache leader.

Geronimo, now 53 years old, strode proudly to meet the Indian police. They awaited him at one end of the rectangular cluster of buildings which made up Warm Springs. Geronimo was followed by nearly 100 warriors carrying army rifles.

"What do you want?" he asked Clum.

"We come with orders to bring you and your renegades back to the San Carlos reservation," Clum said quietly. "You have broken the peace treaty of Cochise. You have killed many whites and you have stolen much livestock."

Geronimo threw his head back and laughed with contempt. "You and your band will arrest me?" he said. "Do not bother me any longer or my warriors will see that you become food for the desert beasts."

The old Indian whirled around to leave, when he heard the sudden sound of rifles cocking. His startled glance lit upon nearly 100 Apache police who had surrounded him. The police had been hiding in the nearby buildings and had crept out as he spoke with Clum. Geronimo's hand flew to the trigger on his rifle, then, staring down the barrels of so many guns, he eased it away and laid down the gun.

The Apache police quickly clapped leg irons on Geronimo and his subchiefs, and they were herded into a wagon and driven to the reservation, 400 miles away. Two weeks later, however, he was released from the guardhouse where he had been held and turned loose on to the reservation. It wasn't long before he had fled the borders of San Carlos, and the dawn rang again with the terrifying cries of his raiding warriors.

"What do you suggest we do, Mr. President?" General George Crook asked quietly. "I trust you have read the reports about Geronimo's continued attacks on Arizona settlers. They are demanding we send more soldiers and that we kill every Apache in the territory.

President Chester Arthur turned from the window in his office toward the soldier addressing him. He indicated that the general should take a seat, and sat himself down at his desk to page through a file

"You say we have had more than 3,000 cavalry men on his trail and we still have not captured him?"

"Yes, Mr. President. He knows the Sierra Madre mountains like the back of his hand, and he is cunning and swift. He also has no fear. He recently raided an army post to get guns and ammunition."

The President closed the file and adjusted his glasses. He leaned back in his chair and looked directly at the general.

"We must make a treaty at once with Mexico. I realize your men have their hands tied not being able to follow him across the border. We will change that. Then, I want you to do everything in your power to stop him. Recruit more Apaches to help you, if you must. I understand many of them do not like Geronimo either."

President Arthur stood up and offered his hand to the soldier. "Good luck, general. As I understand the situation, you will need it."

For nearly half a year, General Crook and his Apache scouts tracked Geronimo and his band. Finally, the pursuit paid off. The day came when Geronimo knew it was over. This realization followed a fierce battle with Crook and his many soldiers. Geronimo's ragged band of warriors were tired and hungry. Many of his people had died, killed either by the white man's bullet or the sheer exhaustion of running.

Geronimo set the surrender talks for two days later in a canyon south of the United States-Mexico border. There, he laid down his arms.

The rickety old wagon rattled on through the darkness toward Fort Sill, Oklahoma, Geronimo's home for the past few years. After surrendering to the whites, he had been sent to a prison camp in Florida, then to one in Alabama and finally to Fort Sill.

On that particular day, he had been to a nearby town where he had traded some toys he had made for a bottle of whiskey. The whiskey was already half gone, used to chase away the chill of the cold rain.

Suddenly the buggy hit a stone in the road. The jolt toppled Geronimo out of the driver's seat onto the muddy road. The horse, not realizing what had happened, continued on its way. The 80-year-old Apache leader was left to die hundreds of miles from the homeland he had worked so hard to protect.

The rain poured down, splattering tiny drops of mud on the once-proud Apache's face. His mind, dulled by the alcohol, began to drift away from the cold and pain to his parents' teachings in the warm, sunny desert.

We will know when the world is to end because there will be no water or rain. All of the people in the world will come to those few springs that remain, and they will fight over the water until they kill each other.

After that, the world will be made new again. Those who were Indian will come back white and those who were white will be Indian.

That is the way it will be.